Ten F
about

Volume Two

Candlestick Press

Published by:

Candlestick Press,
Diversity House, 72 Nottingham Road, Arnold, Nottingham UK NG5 6LF
www.candlestickpress.co.uk

Design and typesetting by Diversity Creative Marketing Solutions Ltd.,
www.diversity.agency

Printed by Ratcliff & Roper Print Group, Nottinghamshire, UK

Selection © Di Slaney, 2017

Introduction © Alison O'Neill, 2017 www.shepherdess.co.uk

Cover illustration © Rob Barnes, 2017 www.robbarnesart.co.uk

Candlestick Press monogram © Barbara Shaw, 2008

© Candlestick Press, 2017
Reprinted 2021

Donation to Rare Breeds Survival Trust www.rbst.org.uk

ISBN 978 1 907598 55 5

Acknowledgements:

The poems in this pamphlet are reprinted from the following books, all by
permission of the publishers listed unless stated otherwise. Every effort has
been made to trace the copyright holders of the poems published in this book.
The editor and publisher apologise if any material has been included without
permission or without the appropriate acknowledgement, and would be glad
to be told of anyone who has not been consulted. Thanks are due to all the
copyright holders cited below for their kind permission:

Alfred Brendel, *Collected Poems of Alfred Brendel: Playing the Human Game*
- Bilingual Edition (Phaidon Press, 2010)

Jim Carruth, *Killochries* (Freight Books, 2015)

Nicola Daly, *Candelabrum Vol. 12, No. 6*, by kind permission of the author

Hannah Lowe, 'The Hitcher' first published in *The Rialto* in 2012, by kind
permission of the author

Hugh McMillan, *Aphrodite's Anorak* (Peterloo Poets, 1996) by kind permission
of the author

Carl Sandburg, *The Complete Poems of Carl Sandburg* (Harcourt Brace
Jovanovich, 1970)

Susan Taylor, *A Small Wave for Your Form* (Oversteps Books Ltd, 2012), by
permission of the author and Oversteps Books

Siriol Troup, *Drowning Up The Blue End* (Bluechrome Publishing, 2004)

All permissions cleared courtesy of Swift Permissions
(swiftpermissions@gmail.com)

Where poets are no longer living, their dates are given.

Introduction

I don't like sheep, I love them and I always have. One of my earliest memories is the smell of warm damp wool, the inside of a large cardboard box and a tiny lamb swaddled in a pink towel. I can still feel the roar of an open fire on my face and how tight, red and tingling my cheeks felt. Our statuesque sheepdog observed every moment through keen but kindly eyes. But the thing I recall most is the heartbeat of the lamb cradled in my arms, how tight I held her and the overwhelming love I felt for this woolly fragile creature. The lamb was stone cold when my father found her that dark night in the mud, far too weak to walk or bleat. The lamb was given to me and I was told if you nurse her and she lives, she is yours.

Shepherding is as much about instinct as it is about nurture and care; it is a profession that chooses you and one of the oldest occupations in the world. Our heritage is of sheep; centuries of dedicated men and women have reared and protected their flocks caring for the diverse landscapes they live and thrive in. Sheep provide us with two things, meat and wool, and many people underestimate their intelligence. Sheep can recognise other sheep, they form strong bonds with some in their flock, and much like humans take dislikes too. They have personalities, emotions and great character, in particular our native breeds, all different in their ways. Sheep know their shepherd and have been known to recall a human face years on. They remember landmarks, trees and rivers and will keep to ancient hefts on unfenced land, passing this knowledge to their offspring. Sheep have allowed me to live a life I always wanted, one of simplicity and splendid solitude, and to them I will be eternally grateful for all they have provided.

It is such a pleasure for me to introduce you to this wonderful volume of sheep poems, all refreshingly different and enjoyable. As a shepherd, I was told by my grandfather never to keep a mixed flock, but within these pages there is a truly mixed flock, and it is a delight: so many types of sheep, ideas and views. For any lover of sheep, this will be a joy to own and keep.

Alison O'Neill

The art of keeping sheep

Most nights she lays awake counting the different breeds.
The rare breeds are her favourites.
She takes care to separate the short wools from the long wools first.
She had never kept anything before sheep, not even a secret.
She just lost sleep counting her clients' money as it floated off the
                                        screen into thin air.
She has recently decided that sheep are more reliable than stocks
                                        and shares.
The crofters are stubborn old hands
Who like rams enjoy butting against her dream to keep sheep.
They don't think she is cut out for country life.
According to the post-mistress she disregards the beasts like biros.
She lets them loose, near narrow lanes,
Whilst she stops to collect bits of fleece off fences.

A pensive woman of sixty who lives next door
Reckons that she has more to learn.
'There is an art to keeping sheep' she says quietly leading her
                                        towards the pens.

Nicola Daly

from **Killochries**

vii. flock master

He whistles on Meg,
calls *Away bye,*
sends her up the hill,

signals a wide arc
to gather up
his treasured flock,

bring them back
to the waiting pens:

shouts commands
sleeping sound
in his chair.

Patience is built wi the wait.
And that is what we have done,
watching the flock these last few days,
eager for the first birth
to kick-start the rest,

laughing at two brown hares
solitary all winter
on their hind legs,
throwing punches.

Happens without fanfare,
one slipping out unnoticed,
soon joined by a twin,
sticky and weak,
both testing their voices,
calling their mother,
who licks them clean with her tongue,
brings them to their feet and feeds them.

And we who are not needed this time
keep our distance.

Jim Carruth

A Very Small Miracle

A lamb was born near Dunnet Head,
tumbling in a yellow broth of legs
on the dark earth,
finding its feet just before
the brawling wind from the skerries did.

Nobody paid much heed.
The ewes were not easily impressed
by gyniatrics, and two old women
talked on about tomatoes.
There wasn't even a farmer there
to count this a triumph for finance.

The dreaming lamb wobbled
on the lip of cold reality.
At thirty seconds old it had felt
the first rough edge of a tongue
and already knew that life
was not a bed of turnips.

At a minute
it was standing quite still
staring rudely at me,
as if it knew that being born
a sheep here,
in these extremes of circumstance,
was a very small miracle indeed.

Hugh McMillan

A sheep

A sheep
addressed me as follows
True
you do not have my looks
my wool my curls
your voice
does not pierce the heart
your speech
fails to convey the essential
you do not run after rams
you love neither peace nor nature
sneeze in July
and disappear
at the slightest trickle of rain
beneath your umbrella

And yet
you remain one of us
Even black sheep do
Underneath your wolf's clothing
something frail and gentle
begs for protection
I salute you
little lamb at the shambles

Baaaah
I said

Alfred Brendel

Sheep

When I write the word *sheep*, a sheep
is what I want you to see, barely a gap
between my sheep and yours.

You'll get – a hieroglyph, woolly
but exact, long-nosed, four-legged, silly
as a … sheep.

Instant communication, pen
to paper, paper to brain –
high-speed magic

fleeced from my top hat. This mammal, grass-
eating, singular, white as snow, is yours.
Mine's a flock

on castors, gliding in shadow
through a waist-high late-August meadow,
a scene out of Blake

or Samuel Palmer: a slow stream
of plural consciousness that roams
my psyche

sheepishly, pausing to ruminate
on the countless nuances between one bleat
and the next.

My archetypal sheep gambol
away down the lane, their bags of wool
unravelling behind

and no matter how fast I run, I can't
catch their threads, can't pen them in, can't
pin them down.

They're not interested in telepathic
intercourse, they chew up semantics
like herbivores.

They graze and shit and sleep. They don't need
words to fill out their contours – all they need is cud
and water,

sky above, a patch of earth below, perhaps
the occasional dip. They *know* what they are –
it's written all over them.

Siriol Troup

from **The Sheep Fold**

ii. Jacobs

They were mother and daughter,
wild as hares,
eyes of molten glass.

They looked out for each other,
wouldn't be confined
to such things as fields.

They were pied like gypsy mares,
ran as fast
as flecked foam on the sea's crest.

An old hand called them breakers.

Susan Taylor

The Calmness of Sheep

The summer I was eighteen I stole a sheep.
It was very late, I'd left a party,
climbed the wet black hill behind the house.
Hands sunk in the sheep's wool, I dragged her through the fields,
her eyes like small moons that looked straight at me,
a gaze I couldn't fathom: as with all animals,
their thoughts are theirs alone.
Soon I let go, walked on, she calmly followed
over hills wrapped in the pale smoke
of dawn. I recalled the sheep I drew as a child,
flocks of faceless clouds on sticks pinned to kitchen walls.

We went on, our solitude unbroken until the first wall,
a road, a house, the sound of a crying child.
Here on the verge we sat and I smoked,
remembering the party and what followed –
how I longed to climb the hill, to be alone.
I could smell the sheep, the warm stench of an animal,
and even now that night comes back to me –
her wool and the wet black fields
that I sometimes watch from this deafening house
where there are always parties
and never the calmness of sheep.

Hannah Lowe

Sheep in Winter

The sheep get up and make their many tracks
And bear a load of snow upon their backs,
And gnaw the frozen turnip to the ground
With sharp quick bite, and then go noising round
The boy that pecks the turnips all the day
And knocks his hands to keep the cold away
And laps his legs in straw to keep them warm
And hides behind the hedges from the storm.
The sheep, as tame as dogs, go where he goes
And try to shake their fleeces from the snows,
Then leave their frozen meal and wander round
The stubble stack that stands beside the ground,
And lie all night and face the drizzling storm
And shun the hovel where they might be warm.

John Clare (1793 – 1864)

Sheep

THOUSANDS of sheep, soft-footed, black-nosed sheep—one by one going up the hill and over the fence—one by one four-footed pattering up and over—one by one wiggling their stub tails as they take the short jump and go over—one by one silently unless for the multitudinous drumming of their hoofs as they move on and go over—thousands and thousands of them in the gray haze of evening just after sundown—one by one slanting in a long line to pass over the hill—

I am the slow, long-legged Sleepyman and I love you sheep in Persia, California, Argentina, Australia, or Spain—you are the thoughts that help me when I, the Sleepyman, lay my hands on the eyelids of the children of the world at eight o'clock every night—you thousands and thousands of sheep in a procession of dusk making an endless multitudinous drumming on the hills with your hoofs.

Carl Sandburg (1878 – 1967)

How the sheep found Bo-Peep

Little Bo-Peep awoke from her sleep,
  Her eyes opened wide and wider,
For she found herself seated on the grass
  With an old sheep standing beside her.

"Little Bo-Peep," said the good, old sheep,
  "How glad I am we've found you!
"Here we are—rams and sheep and lambs—
  "All flocking up around you."

"You blessed sheep," said little Bo-Peep,
  "I've been worried to death about you."
"We've been searching for you," said the good old sheep,
  "We wouldn't go home without you."

Eugene Field (1850 – 1895)